Love Travels Forever

Jaye Frances

Redstone Press Media
ISBN 978-0692541913
Printed in the United States of America
www.JayeFances.com

Notes from the Author

Love Travels Forever is a collection of seventeen short stories and essays, many of which have been previously published in abbreviated versions. Magazines are notoriously restrictive in the amount of space they can afford to dedicate to an article, and publishers often request that a writer reduce or otherwise edit a story to fit a specific space requirement.

It's the nature of the beast. Think of it as a balancing act—there are only so many pages, and each one must be used to maximize both income and reader interest.

In *Love Travels Forever*, I've been able to expand, or in some cases restore many of the pieces to their original length and content.

Table of Contents

Love Travels Forever

There's something special about planning a vacation. Whether it's a cruise to the Caribbean or a hike into the Grand Canyon, the anticipation of exploring new destinations and discovering jaw-dropping scenery fires the imagination with the promise of new experiences and the possibility of making new friends.

Many times, pictures of idyllic white-sand beaches, cotton candy sunsets, and swaying palm trees become the recipe for a second honeymoon, when the obligations and responsibilities of everyday living can be left behind to enjoy some uninterrupted time with your spouse.

Typically, we begin the process by perusing resort websites and travel brochures. We read the schedules, check the itineraries and, if budget and timing allow, make the reservations, looking forward to the departure date like a child counts down the days to Christmas.

More often than not, however, we set our travel plans aside and return to the more practical side of life, telling ourselves that *some day* we're going to try that new resort in Mexico, or spend a week relaxing on a cruise ship in the Caribbean or Mediterranean.

Bottom line, we seldom associate a sense of urgency with our travel plans. We consider the comfortable accommodations, the activities, and the new sights we'll see as luxuries, while making the assumption that the future will always hold the same possibilities and opportunities.

But life has a beginning—and an end.

It's one of those irrefutable facts that none of us like to think about. And for a forty-five-year-old man named Evan, it became a reality much too soon.

I met Evan on a Caribbean cruise out of Ft. Lauderdale. We were both browsing in the onboard gift ship when he approached and asked for my opinion about a tie he was considering. He'd forgotten to pack one and the recommended dress for the dining room that evening was formal. After he'd chosen the conservative dark blue, we chatted about the usual topics—where we were from, the ship's itinerary, and what we thought of the food.

"Are you traveling with family?" I asked.

He hesitated, as if not sure how to answer. Finally, he offered a resigned smile and said, "Yes, I suppose in a way, I am."

I resisted my natural curiosity. My questions would extend beyond the boundaries of polite conversation. He must have seen the confusion on my face because he immediately offered an explanation and in doing so, shared one of the most moving and powerful memories a surviving spouse can have—the last time they traveled with their soul mate.

He called it their "goodbye cruise," and even though his wife—Frankie—had been gone for four years, he described their last journey together with such detail and emotion, it was easy to imagine it could have happened last week.

They had received the news from the doctor without warning. It didn't seem possible—the prognosis, the short time that remained. And when the oncologist began talking about a treatment schedule, Frankie had wanted to wait. There was something else she wanted to do—something more important.

A cruise. Together.

It was a trip they had often promised each other they would take. But for reasons that are all too familiar, they had put it off, postponing what was now the most important thing in her life—a life now measured in days instead of years.

"During the first half of the cruise, Frankie was so excited. She reveled in the quick kisses on the dance floor, the secret scoot of the proper piece of silverware as the next dinner course was served, and the short strolls we took down secluded stretches of beach. But by midweek, I noticed she was walking the decks a bit more slowly, and in the evenings, she wanted to turn in early, right after dinner.

"The last three days of the trip, she was too tired to sit through a meal in the dining room, so we had our food served in our cabin. But we were never lonely—the friends we made on board would always drop by and check on us. A soft knock on the door and Frankie's eyes would brighten, and then she would flood them with questions: 'What color were the flowers in the table centerpiece? Which tour excursions did you take? Did you swim in the ocean or just walk along the shore?'

"Occasionally, someone would make a comment about a particular restaurant or activity being so enjoyable that it would definitely be on the list to do again, on their next cruise. And then there was a sudden silence as everyone remembered that re-visiting the same destination was not an option for my precious Frankie."

Evan paused as he saw the tears gathering in my eyes. He reached out and took my hand. "So now," he continued, "I take the same cruise every two years, reliving the moments and memories—the times when we walked hand-in-hand along the beach or when we asked for a breakfast table just for two, and especially when we watched the islands pass from our balcony, talking about what it would be like to live there . . . for the rest of our lives.

"The first time I traveled alone—that first trip after Frankie was gone—was very hard. But now I can almost feel her sitting next to me, or standing close by on the deck. And even though I miss her like hell, I really believe she wants me to be here."

We hugged. We cried. And as we parted, he left me with a special wish: "Don't wait for tomorrow," he said. "Live now. Travel now.

Fill your lives with the joy of new people and places while you are together. Even if you can't take that big trip, just spending three to four weekends a year with the love of your life is better than a once-in-a-lifetime vacation that never happens because, for one of you, a lifetime just wasn't long enough."

It was a difficult story to hear, and an even more difficult one to write. But it was a story full of love and compassion and it echoed the wisdom of the old adage, 'You never know how much someone means to you until you lose them.'

My chance meeting with Evan was an incredible gift, reminding me of how fortunate I am to have my soul mate by my side. Yet I also know that life changes with the seasons. And if one day I find myself navigating this world alone, I will remember my visit with

Evan and be grateful for his unwavering spirit, and especially for his story about two hearts and a love that travels forever.

A Valentine for Danny

I'd like to share my favorite Valentine's story. It's about a twenty-two-year-old woman named Wanda, and how she helped hundreds of couples celebrate Valentine's Day—every day of the year.

During World War II, Wanda worked at the Fayetteville, North Carolina train station selling tickets, making reservations, and helping passengers locate their luggage.

Trains ran full in those days, and getting a ticket without an advance reservation could mean waiting on a hard bench for hours, until the next train traveling in your direction had an empty seat or someone with a reservation didn't show up.

Servicemen on leave seldom had reservations. Traveling on a weekend pass, they took the chance of getting a coveted ticket, hoping to see their family for a day or two before they had to make the trip back. Unfortunately for many soldiers, their passes were spent entirely in the station, sleeping on wooden benches, waiting for a cancellation that never came. And because Fayetteville was home to Fort Bragg, the largest training facility during WWII, many of the boys were only days away from being shipped overseas. Being able to get a seat on the train meant seeing their family, wives, and sweethearts one last time—until the war was over.

During the first few weeks at her job, Wanda saw how disappointing it was for soldiers who had to watch train after train leave the station, not knowing if the next one would have an available seat. A service-wife herself—her husband stationed overseas—

Wanda also knew firsthand how difficult it was for the waiting wives and family watching the trains pull in, praying their loved one was on board, and hoping they would be able to spend a few precious hours together.

One morning, Wanda noticed a soldier standing expectantly to the side of her window. The red stub of numbered paper between his fingers meant he was on the standby list. She also noticed that under his arm were two small tins of candy, both tied with identical red bows. And while the ribbons were a bit worse for wear, it was obvious he was trying to keep them from being crushed.

After the next scheduled train pulled out from the station—without him—the soldier stepped up to Wanda's window and politely asked if there was any chance of getting on the next one. She explained that since projected passenger and seat counts were often in error, the conductor would have to actually check the number of vacant seats after the next train arrived. Until then, she had no way of knowing.

He smiled and thanked her, and then stepped off to the side to wait.

By the time Wanda was ready for her break, the soldier had moved to one of the benches next to the window overlooking the boarding platform. As she often did, Wanda walked through the waiting room with her cup of tea, checking on the passengers and reassuring the wait-listed—especially the soldiers—that she was doing everything she could to get them on the next departure. Occasionally, she would sit down next to one of the servicemen and spend a few minutes chatting, usually about his hometown or his plans for after the war.

Wanda told me they were always great stories, but the ones she remembered most were about the sweethearts and wives that were waiting. She said she often imagined her husband telling a very similar story, whenever someone was considerate enough to ask, and kind enough to listen.

Since this particular soldier looked as tired as he was anxious, Wanda wasn't sure he would appreciate her company. But as she walked by, he immediately invited her to sit next to him and finish her tea. After the young man introduced himself, Wanda learned that "Danny" had recently completed basic training and would be shipped overseas in five days. The night before, he had called his girlfriend—Peggy—and asked her to be his wife. If he could manage to get home today, they would have just enough time to find a

Justice of the Peace and spend one day together as a married couple before he had to return to his unit.

Wanda's break ended far too soon, and as she shook Danny's hand, she asked about the two boxes of candy. "One's for my girl," he said. "The other one is for my mom."

Wanda silently swore she would get Danny on the next train.

She took her position behind the window and her supervisor handed her the stack of banded tickets for the next departure. After carefully counting them, she found there were 31 available seats. But the number of reserved passengers, plus those wait-listed with lower numbers than Danny's, totaled over forty.

With as much courage as she could muster, and after turning around to make sure no one was watching, Wanda pulled the bottom ticket from the stack and slipped it under the cash drawer. She knew if she were discovered it would mean her job—a job she couldn't afford to lose.

After waiting for the call to board, she motioned to Danny to come to her window. As she pressed the ticket into his hand, she whispered that a "cancellation" had just opened up a seat, and then shook her head and smiled, a signal that he wasn't to say anything. He slid a few folded bills across the counter and nodded. Turning to leave, he hesitated long enough to slip one of the boxes of candy into Wanda's hands. Before she could say anything, he was outside on the platform, and in seconds had disappeared into the nearest passenger car.

The date was February 14, 1942.

From that day on, Wanda always tried to pull a single ticket from each train's final seat allocation—not stealing it, but saving it— waiting for the opportunity to place it into the hands of a hopeful soldier.

A good day for Wanda was getting one or two servicemen on board and headed home to see their wife or sweetheart. A great day was four or five.

I asked Wanda how many boys she was able to put on those trains. She told me she didn't know for sure, but "it was quite a few." I estimate that during the two years she worked at the station, it had to be in the hundreds.

And yes, Wanda's husband finally returned from the war. He arrived on one of the very same trains that had carried so many other soldiers home for the weekend—a weekend that never would have happened without Wanda.

As I said in the beginning, Wanda's story has always been one of my favorites. And while obviously biased, I'm also certain it's true—because Wanda was my grandmother. And if she were alive today, I'm sure Valentine's Day would still be her favorite holiday.

On The First Day of Spring

They arrive wrapped in welcome sunshine—drifting clouds, soaring kites, and cherry blossoms. All promises of spring, bringing with them a sense of growth and renewal, of rejuvenation and revival and, according to Alfred Lord Tennyson, "thoughts of love."

Spring has traditionally been a time to celebrate our relationships, to rekindle the spark of passion and intimacy. And while the popularized example of an April love usually focuses on the young and their quest for a new romantic interest, it's equally important to commemorate the existing relationship we have with our spouse or significant other. For most couples, a good marriage and relationship equates to a great life.

Last month, I met a wonderful couple who, many years ago, took the rites of spring to heart. Their poignant story about commitment, devotion, and a personal love ritual they celebrate every year was very touching. I hope you'll find their example as inspiring as I did.

Henry and Alice were married on March 21, 1961, just two months before graduating from Arizona State University. That summer, Henry was hired by Mountain Bell and was looking forward to quick promotions and success in the corporate world. But within eight months he received his draft notice, and after completing basic training, Henry was assigned to the Campbell base in Heidelberg, Germany. He and Alice decided that she would stay in Arizona—close to her parents—and visit Henry as often as possible.

Leaving Alice behind was one of the hardest things Henry had ever done, and before he deployed for overseas duty, they celebrated their first anniversary. That night, he took Alice by the hand and repeated their wedding vows, adding that if he could do it over again, he would "marry her in a New York minute."

Two years later, Henry completed his military service and returned to his job at Mountain Bell, working rotating shifts as a central office technician while Alice struggled through her first pregnancy. Money was tight, and she did her best to help out by baking wedding cakes for one of the local reception halls.

Through the years, they experienced the predictable and the unforeseen, and yet they never forgot their first anniversary ritual. And although their second anniversary had to be shared by telephone, it was the only one they celebrated apart. Every following March 21st, after Alice had cleared away the dishes and they had opened each other's card, they took each other's hand and repeated their vows, words they now knew by heart.

This March, Alice and Henry will recite their wedding vows for the 50th time.

During our recent visit, I asked them if they would share their secret to a happy marriage. They looked at each other and laughed.

"I suppose it's a lot like a prescription," Henry began. "It changes for what ails you. Sometimes, it's an equal dose of tenacity and patience. Other times, it's simply being there, supporting each other when life throws you a curve ball. If there's anything we've learned about having a successful marriage, it's simply deciding, each day when you wake up, that there's no other person you'd rather be with. You commit to each other because you know how important your relationship is, and how much better your life is because of it."

We continued to chat for another hour, with Henry and Alice recalling memories of their first real vacation together, the births of their two children, and the time they were pulling a travel trailer cross-country and Henry drove away from a gas station leaving Alice inside the Texaco restroom. ("I really thought she was in the trailer," he said. "I never saw her get out to use the bathroom.")

Although Henry and Alice continued to good-naturedly dismiss the value of any specific advice that they might share with other couples, I gained a great deal of insight from our conversation. And so from their stories, memories, and remembrances, here's what I learned:

- There are no mind readers. Your spouse needs to know your expectations. When you find yourself upset or unhappy, explain to your mate why some situations and behaviors leave you disappointed and, more important, what could have been done to prevent it. By the same token, listen to your spouse when he or she needs the same consideration. Healthy relationships do not spring from movie magic and romance novels.

- Support your partner with everything you've got. Make your spouse's happiness and well-being a priority. Put them first in your life and see what happens. Build your future together with mutual goals. And if you sense that you're pulling ahead or away from your spouse, talk about it and, if necessary, readjust how you're spending your time. Value each other as you would a priceless work of art—keeping it safe and protected for as long as it is entrusted to you.

- Don't let the intensity fade. New relationships are full of highs and lows, but over time, familiarity and the general consistency of life tend to even out our emotions. And while that means the disappointments are generally less devastating, it can also mean the feelings of excitement can become little more than a memory. It's easy—and unhealthy—to take your spouse for granted. Remind yourself of the dedication, companionship, and contentment they provide. Try to imagine how much you would miss them—what your life would be like without them.

- Cultivate common interests. We've all heard that opposites attract, but it just isn't true. For long-term happiness, it's important to develop and nurture mutual interests. Explore things you like to do together, even if it means learning a new skill or activity that both can participate in.

- It's the little things. When Henry and Alice described the best parts of their lives, they never mentioned the new car they were driving or the several homes they had bought and lived in, or even the accomplishments they achieved in their careers. They reminisced about the little things: Sitting together on a porch swing, walking in the rain, having a picnic on a Saturday afternoon—the kind of memories that are made by spending simple times together without worrying about the future or fretting over the past. Strive to find quiet moments you can share, without the distractions and demands of career and material accomplishments.

As Henry and Alice began to leave, I asked them if they had any regrets, if there was anything they would do differently if they had the chance.

Alice answered without hesitation. "I look back on our memories the same way I think about an old blanket we received as a wedding gift. Although it's faded and a little threadbare—"

"Kind of like us," Henry interjected with a chuckle.

Alice gave her husband a quick wink and continued, "I still reach down and pull it over us every night just before we go to sleep. I would miss that blanket if it wasn't there. And

I can't image what our life would be like if we tried to change a single moment of the past."

As I watched them drive away, I realized Henry and Alice were another perennial promise of spring, but contrary to Tennyson, *their* "thoughts of love" were good for all seasons.

An American Valentine

He was good-looking, smart, and athletic. And unlike the other boys on the football team who were always spouting pretentious drivel about themselves, Joey displayed a kind of quiet assurance—almost shyness—that quickly made him the focus of my burgeoning fourteen-year-old-libido.

I loved him. At least that's what I told myself the second week of my freshman year. Consumed with the heart-tugging fever of love-at-first-sight, I'd done everything but outright declare my less-than-innocent adoration to his face.

I made sure we sat at the same lunch table in the cafeteria. I offered—and he occasionally accepted—my invitation to study together.

And although our conversation always flowed fast and easy—chatting about our teachers, the game coming up on Friday (and the dance afterward)—the topic of "us" was carefully avoided.

Although I was curious, I never knew much about Joey's family until a seemingly innocent question opened a window into his past. It was on one of those Mondays following a big game weekend. I was characteristically gushing over him, telling him how well he'd played, and I commented about how proud his parents must have been to watch him on the field. He told me his mother worked nights and had never seen a single game.

"What about your dad?" I asked. "He was probably there, right?"

He fell quiet and looked away for several seconds. At first I thought he might be embarrassed about his father's appearance—maybe his weight, or the way he dressed.

"My father isn't here anymore." He said it softly, but with enough emotion that I realized he wasn't taking about a divorced parent living in a different city. I was surprised when he volunteered the details. "He was killed in Vietnam . . . a long time ago. I was really young."

I felt awkward. I wanted to say something meaningful, something that would make a difference. The best I could offer was, "Oh, I didn't know," and "I'm sorry." Both so completely inadequate.

We sat together on one of the benches in the quad for nearly a minute, not speaking. Finally, he reached into his pocket and retrieved a small piece of triangle-shaped fabric. About three-by-five inches, it was dark green with a black horse-head at the top and a diagonal line running across it.

"It's from his uniform. I carry it with me, until I can put it on mine."

I wasn't exactly sure what Joey meant, so I nodded, hoping he wouldn't think I was shallow and uncaring for wanting to change the subject.

The fall turned to winter, the Christmas season came and went, and as the second semester started, the affection I had for Joey had grown even stronger. Yet *his* attention remained focused on grades and sports. By the first of February, I couldn't stand it. I decided it was time to reveal my feelings, and there would be no better opportunity than on Valentine's Day.

For the next two weeks, I compared hand-made cards to store-bought. I composed a dozen lines of prose, working on it for days until it became a pledge of passion, dedicating my heart and soul to the only boy I was sure I would ever love. Finally, I was ready.

On the morning of the fourteenth, I waited by Joey's locker, trying to stay calm, occasionally shuffling back and forth to the drinking fountain and hoping I didn't appear as obvious as I felt. When I saw him at the end of the hallway, I held my breath, struggling to keep my stomach from doing flip-flops. As he moved closer, he returned my awkward smile with a nod. I took it as an invitation.

"Happy Valentine's Day, Joey." I pushed the card out in front of me, as if I were jousting with a piece of paper.

I waited. Would he reach out, take my hand and hold it while he slipped the card he'd brought for me between my fingers? Or would he pause and lock his eyes with mine, telling me how special I was to think of him?

In a grabbing flash, Joey snatched the envelope from my hand and tossed it into the recesses of his locker. "Thanks." It sounded like an afterthought, the kind of token appreciation offered by a faceless fast-food employee working the drive-through window. He turned and closed his locker, but not before I glanced inside and noticed the large stack of cards he'd already collected—and mine, now unceremoniously added to the growing pile. With a quick "See ya," he was on his way to his first class.

I stood there, devastated. As embarrassment quickly replaced disappointment, I looked around, wondering how many of my friends had seen his reckless abandonment of my feelings.

The walk home from school was torture. My girlfriends were chatting about the cards they had received. Naturally, Joey's name was at the top of the list. "I got one. How 'bout you? Did yours have a little set of smiling hearts or was it different?"

I told them I hadn't opened mine yet, suggesting it wasn't that important to me. I tried to convince them that the whole idea of exchanging cards on Valentine's Day was juvenile, something we should leave in our childhood because, after all, we were almost adults now.

That evening I moped through dinner, ignored the television, and pretended to do my homework. I had no idea how I would face Joey the next day. Inside my card I had included a short poem—a proclamation of my unconditional love and devotion. Now it read like the epitaph on a fool's grave.

"Did you find the letters I put on your dresser?" My mother was finishing the dinner dishes. No longer distracted by mealtime conversation, she had remembered the two pieces of mail.

I wondered. It seemed much too formal, too grown up, to send a Valentine through the mail. Especially for a fifteen-year-old. I headed to my room, picked up the envelopes, and scanned the return addresses. The first was from my older sister—no doubt an epistle of sibling superiority detailing her escapades of living in a college dorm. I tossed it aside to be opened later. The remaining envelope hinted of currency, with two pieces of card stock undoubtedly disguising the real contents. With just a P.O. Box as a return address, I reasoned it was probably a card from the family gypsy, my wandering uncle, who thought of me as another obligation to be settled with a five-dollar bill. I started to lay it back on the dresser, then reasoned if it *was* money, I could use it to pick up the math binder I needed.

I ripped open the envelope. At first glance, I dismissed the possibility of a cash windfall; in fact, I wasn't sure what was inside. Even after removing the contents from between the folded construction paper, I still didn't understand. Finally, as I ran my fingers across the embroidered fabric, I recognized the shoulder patch Joey had pulled from his pocket months ago. Along with the patch, he had included a simple note: "*I wish I had known him better. I was only five when he died, but from reading his letters, I think you would have liked my dad. I know he would have liked you."* He signed it, *"Love, Joey."*

Like most young loves, Joey and I were never destined to be soul mates. Instead, we quickly evolved into best friends— encouraging, comforting, and supporting each other as we shared the joys and disappointments of adolescence.

I kept the patch for three years, until I mailed it to Ft. Benning, Georgia, where Joey began his military training. Four years later he brought it back to me, when I stood beside his mother to welcome him home from the Persian Gulf War. As I put my arms around him, I noticed his father's patch had been added to his uniform, right under the shoulder sleeve insignia of his own unit—the First Cavalry Division. They were identical, except for the color. His father's was green—made to be less conspicuous in the jungles of Vietnam—while Joey's reflected the tan background of Desert Storm.

They were simple embroidered patches of cloth, yet they represented a family legacy of commitment, service, and sacrifice. And they also meant my first real Valentine had finally come home—where he belonged.

It's All a Matter of Choice

I was reading a business article a couple of weeks ago, and I noticed the writer using the phrase, "being comfortable in your own skin." I wondered why such a widely-read business author would use such a trite and overused metaphor.

Made popular years ago, the expression encouraged an attitude of acceptance, promoting a guiltless surrender to flaws and imperfections in physical appearance. Over time, the axiom evolved into a popular way of defining a state of personal authenticity—creating a sense of flow in our lives, of doing things in a way that made the most sense, even when our choices departed from the traditional.

After a little research, I learned the phrase is on the verge of making a comeback. Perhaps it's time. Seems like every ten years, the self-help industry checks the recycle bin for second-hand concepts that can be re-packaged into books and seminars for the next generation. So with the latest re-issue of "finding a personal comfort zone" pre-eminently upon us, I'd like to make a suggestion: Let's include a context that goes far beyond the reluctant acceptance of situations and issues beyond our control. Let's make it about the celebration of choice.

Since I often share personal experiences with readers, I'd like to offer an example that is near and dear to my heart. A few months ago, my husband and I celebrated our eighteenth wedding anniversary. But unlike the customary observance, we *renewed* our desire to continue our relationship for another year. It's something we've done since our first anniversary, seventeen years ago. And while not the traditional box of candy and Hallmark card, it's a commemoration of truth, of looking back on the years that we've shared together and deciding the future is better with each other than without.

To me, it's a nearly overwhelming concept—having that choice, even though I would never choose otherwise. It's a part of commitment, maybe the most important part. We are together because we *want* to be. And we make that choice every December.

Unorthodox? Perhaps. But our example pales in comparison to the choices others have made, willingly and without hesitation.

An acquaintance of mine had a fairytale start in life. Born into a loving and financially-secure family, he followed the role models of his parents, attending the best schools, excelling at sports as well as scholastics. After graduation, he moved up the corporate ladder and became a successful executive. At age thirty, he married the girl of his dreams. She was beautiful, intelligent, and supportive of his career. And as they stood before a packed church repeating their wedding vows, most couldn't help but envy them.

The first two years were idyllic for the couple, and while there were adjustments—moving to a new state, making new friends, and coping with the demands of an upwardly-mobile corporate career path—they were, in the most real sense, truly happy.

It was on a quick trip to tour a property that had just come on the market—their potential dream home—that Janice suddenly felt dizzy. Although she told Mark she was fine, she fainted in the car on the way home. She dismissed it, passing it off as a benign symptom of fatigue, probably caused by a lack of sleep from a recent whirlwind trip to Barbados.

Two days later, while Janice was busy in the kitchen preparing a snack for a visiting neighbor, she fell to the floor, unconscious.

Mark stayed by her hospital bed for three days, hoping—praying—that Janice would open her eyes. He knew the doctor's prognosis wasn't good. She had suffered a stroke on the left side of her brain, potentially affecting her memory and the muscle control of the right side of her body.

Her recovery was long and arduous—and incomplete. Even after several years of therapy, she remained confined to a wheelchair and experienced difficulty remembering her home address and phone number.

The misfortune brought a spontaneous outpouring of compassion from family and friends. It was a natural reaction to an unexpected tragedy. But then something unusual happened. After a year or so, after the shock of the event had subsided and people came to accept Janice's situation as an unfortunate happenstance of life, they directed their sympathy—*and pity*—toward Mark. Some even saw him as the victim, denied his rightful destiny because of the "obligation" of being forced to care for his invalid wife.

I remember one of the comments as especially insensitive: "I hate to say it, but she's an albatross around his neck, keeping him from realizing his true potential."

Thankfully, Mark never heard it, at least not directly.

Mark *had* made changes in his priorities. Instead of staying on the fast-track to a vice-presidency of a Fortune 500 company, he asked to be demoted to a less demanding staff position, which would have eliminated the need to travel. The company fired him.

He could have felt sorry for himself, bemoaning his sudden reversal of fortune. After all, he had worked hard, sacrificing his personal interests to concentrate on career advancement and future financial success. Instead, Mark found an on-line sales rep job, allowing him to work from home while he cared for Janice.

While others assumed his decision to change his priorities—and his life—to be a no-win obligation, Mark didn't see it that way. "I always had choices," he said. "But leaving Janice in the hands of strangers was never one of them. I was familiar with corporate titles, and how the business world uses them to motivate, reward, and establish responsibility. It made me realize there were only a few titles that really mattered. So in my way of thinking, I simply added the title of caregiver to my previous status of soul mate."

Mark's courage in a seemingly impossible situation made me realize that many of the so-called obligations in our lives are simply the result of personal choice—whether we realize it or not. Regardless of the situation or circumstances, no one else is going to live our lives for us, which places the responsibility of choosing honestly—and wisely—directly on us.

Turning obligations into choices—I think it's what Mary Ann Evans, writing as George Eliot, was talking about when she said, "The strongest principle of growth lies in human choice."

When Every Saturday Was Father's Day

I recently enjoyed lunch with an old high school friend—one of those rare individuals I've stayed in touch with throughout the thirty-year span of time that separates me from my adolescence. As Ronnie and I reminisced about growing up together in a small town, he asked me if there was one special memory from my youth that stood out from all the others—one that, given the opportunity to relive, I would choose without hesitation.

Instead of feeling overwhelmed with the challenge of selecting a single experience from an overabundance of possibilities, his question stirred a whisper from the past, a memory wrapped in a magical sense of wonder. It took me back to a time before dating and school

49

dances, before peer pressure made friends the preferred companions over parents—a time when I was my daddy's little girl.

My dad often held two jobs, taking on additional work to keep food on the table and make sure the mortgage was paid. It left him with few opportunities to spend time with me, and yet he still found a way—every Saturday morning.

Getting up early to eat breakfast out with my father had become a Saturday tradition. Waking up at six-thirty was definitely not my idea of the perfect way to start the weekend, but my father would always ask. And knowing how much it meant to him—to spend that hour together—I would go.

We always went to the same place, a popular little restaurant with cracked stucco walls and faded yellow paint. The unpaved parking lot added its own flavor to the culinary experience, generating a dust-cloud with each new arrival and departure.

Outside, the thick, sweet aroma of cooking grease laced the air, and although I was still half-asleep, it was hard to ignore the drifting hints of crispy home fries and fresh hot donuts.

It was a busy place, with plates, glasses, and conversation being constantly shuffled back-and-forth across faded green tabletops pock-marked with burn craters from forgotten cigarettes. In the back corner, an old Wurlitzer filled the smoky air with Hank Williams, Tennessee Ernie Ford, and Tammy Wynette—the waitresses often joining in on the chorus as they swished in and out of the kitchen, carrying eggs and bacon, stacks of pancakes, and homemade pie.

We always sat at the counter. Perched on a backless rotating stool, I'd lean over the speckled beige Formica—still wet from the last wipe-down—and sip milk while watching my dad drink coffee from a thick-walled brown mug.

I knew the menu by heart. Typed on a half-sheet of light yellow paper and slid vertically between two pieces of stitched plastic, the only thing that ever changed was the prices, and then only by a nickel or two at the most.

My father ordered two eggs, over easy. He liked the yokes runny. I never heard him order anything else. I usually asked for the same, but well done, with hash browns and toast. The bill came to a buck seventy for both of us. After paying the tab, he always slid the thirty cents change under his plate, even though he said a quarter would have been plenty.

While we sat there, he would talk to me. Sometimes he told me about his job and the people he worked with. Other times he talked about the changes he planned on making around the house. Not big changes, just a new rose bush to replace the one that died or trying a different color of trim on the garage door. And while I'm sure there were times when he struggled for the right words—words that I would understand—I always listened.

There were other conversations going on around us, and occasionally I'd overhear someone say how cute it was to see a father taking his little girl out to breakfast. And more than once, I heard a shallow or misguided comment about how my dad "probably wished I had been born a boy."

But I knew better.

I knew my dad enjoyed my company. There was something special about the bond between us. Something so special it was difficult for him to express, at least in a way that would make sense to a ten-year-old. So he tried to show me, by taking me to breakfast on Saturday mornings. While most of the other men in the restaurant sat with their sons, he proudly sat with his daughter. And when he introduced me, he did it with a strong voice and a ring of pride that was obvious—even to me.

We shared that hour together every Saturday, until I turned thirteen and decided it wasn't "cool" to be seen with my parents in public. What would my girlfriends think? They certainly didn't go out to breakfast with their fathers. So I became a teenager—not rebellious, but wanting to fit in—and like most of my generation, I succumbed to peer pressure.

I think my dad knew it would happen. He realized I was growing up, and soon I would find other interests, other distractions that I would find more interesting, more important than spending time with him on a Saturday morning.

And when it was time, he let me go.

Long after I had left home and married, he continued to eat breakfast on Saturdays at that little restaurant. And even after all these years, I still think about those mornings when he ate alone, surrounded by other men, some of whom I'm sure still sat with their sons, talking about football or the grandchild that was on the way or which brand of beer to bring to the picnic. And I wonder if, just before he left the house, he took a moment to look into my room, to stare at the empty, perfectly-made bed, and then silently ask himself: *Is she okay? Does she need anything? Is this the day she's going to call?*

The old restaurant is still there. My dad is not.

And so, Ronnie, there *is* one memory that outshines all the others. More than any Christmas or birthday, more than any other celebration of my youth, I cherish an early Saturday morning ritual, when my dad and I sat side-by-side on wobbly bar stools and ate an eighty-five-cent breakfast together. Because no matter how many years he's been gone, or how old I become, I'll always be my daddy's little girl.

A Love For Summer

They are the treasures of summers past—picnics by the lake, family vacations, fireworks on the fourth, and cookouts on the beach. All staples of the season. As I sift through these summer touchstones of my youth, I find most of my recollections have been tempered by time, the details faded with age. And yet there is one memory that always transcends the years with perfect clarity, still stirring the emotions and warming the heart—my first summer love.

Maybe it's because summer brought its own special kind of aphrodisiac—the brevity of clothes, the freedom from school, and the potential for romance. It was a heady combination, and beneath it all simmered the unspoken hope of finding a love for all seasons.

Like most, my first summer crush was an experience that predated a loss of innocence, before dating was a regular weekend occurrence, when we could only imagine what it would be like for our lips to touch another's for the first time, and when we reveled in the thought of walking hand-in-hand with someone new.

Perhaps the adolescents of today are too sophisticated, too exposed to the casual-sex attitude promoted by popular media to understand this, but a large part of growing up in the seventies in mid-western America meant spending the early teen years plagued with the ache of anticipation. With our childhoods—and the culture—still influenced by a decade of watching Annette and Frankie linger under a coconut palm, restraint was still the standard for "respectable" girls. And while it may seem conservative by contemporary standards of sexual conduct, for some of us, the fantasy of a yet-to-be-experienced first kiss was magic. So if you're a youngster under thirty-five, read this with patience, the kind that was common forty years ago when personal choice and limits were as popular as hip-hugger bell bottoms, mood rings, and polyester.

My first date was a very secretive affair, even to the point of arranging to meet him inside the movie theater to avoid the possibility of anyone seeing us walk in together. At thirteen, I wasn't willing to risk the interrogation and lecture that was certain to result if my overly protective mother found out I would be spending several hours in the dark with a tempting boy-hunk one year my senior.

My mom was convinced that all 14-year-old boys were minions of the devil, hell-bent on coercing innocent little girls into engaging in all sorts of unspeakable acts, not the least vile of which included touch-dancing and—dare I say it—the goodnight kiss. (She would always grimace at this point, as if I should expect the taste of a boy's lips to be as sour as a slice of lemon.)

My date—I'll call him Nick—had arrived first and saved me a seat. We exchanged a quick "hello," and then silence. While not awkward, it was obvious we didn't have a lot to say to each other. Besides, we could always talk on the phone. And as far as I knew, dates weren't for talking. Dates were supposed to be kisses and hugs and gentle touches, without having to wonder what you would say after your lips parted.

Previews of coming attractions filled the screen. It was official—our date had begun. As we sat there, shoulders apart, arms separated by the tiniest air gap on the armrest, I told myself I was ready.

The show droned on. We ate popcorn and drank soda. I stole an occasional glance, watching him, waiting for a cue.

By the end of the movie, I was aching to feel his arm around me. But as the yellow-orange sunset froze on the screen and the final theme music began to play, he turned toward me and said something about his brother waiting for him. Then without the slightest hesitation, he rose from his seat and left me in the dark, his exit punctuated by a quick, bobbing trace-shadow of his head as it momentarily intercepted the beam of light streaming from the projector.

As the credits rolled, I realized my hopes of creating a few cherished memories had come to an abrupt end. While it's true my expectations were a bit vague and ambiguous, I had hoped going dutch on the purchase of overpriced, greasy popcorn and a watered-down Coke would have produced more favorable results.

Although I didn't realize it then, I had just received an introduction to the awkward and confusing world of dating, with all its passion and heartache, apprehension and disappointment, and where most beginnings inevitably fade into forgettable endings. Those early summer crushes and puppy loves delivered important lessons and, in affairs of the heart, there is simply no better way to learn.

So what happened to Nick? Did I get another chance to explore the possibilities? I did. Even though I kept my feelings a secret, I continued to nurture my hopeful expectations. Three years later, as a fresh-faced sixteen-year-old, I often daydreamed about our first physical encounter, my over-active imagination placing him on the crest of a perfect wave, the water carrying him within a few yards of where I waited on crystal white sand, ready for him to take me in his arms. All that summer—between my junior and senior year—I dreamed of such a coupling and how I would lie there, perfectly still, as the glow from my body illuminated his hard-chiseled features.

Our eventual union was a far cry from my romanticized illusions, but it brought a much-needed dose of reality to my quixotic and starry-eyed notions. And while I still cherish the brief and never-repeated encounter, not once did I ever imagine Nick—captain of the football team, Thespian's member, and owner of a midnight blue 1973 Z-28 Camaro—growing up to become a Dolly Madison route driver, destined to spend the next 30 years of his life restocking grocery shelves with Wonder Bread and Hostess Twinkies.

And that's the point. Even though our adolescent fantasies seldom measure up to what life has in store for us, the summers of our youth gave us hope, a time to consider the possibilities, to experience life as a great adventure instead of a calculated consequence—when a first kiss was served up as a question, begging for an answer.

Looking back, my only regret is that I didn't live the other nine months of the year with the same abandon. But then I wonder . . . is it ever too late?

All The Same Color
Under God's Sun

Last summer, I returned to one of my favorite vacation spots, the island of St. Martin. Ready to savor the sun, sand, and ocean, I checked into the same little beach hotel I've stayed in at least a dozen times since discovering this unique piece of paradise over twenty years ago.

Midweek, the weather changed. A tropical storm was brushing the Lesser Antilles, bringing clouds and light rain to most of the island. As the sky quickly turned from blue to gray, I decided to forgo my original plan to do some snorkeling. Instead, I grabbed an umbrella and headed for the quaint shops, boutiques, and restaurants of Phillipsburg, a picturesque harbor town on the Dutch side of the island.

My first stop was my favorite cosmetics store. Once inside, the sales clerk—a lovely middle-aged, dark-skinned woman named Rinda—approached with an offer to help. As I looked over the shades of lipstick, we chatted about the local economy, the lack of tourists that season, and where to find the best fish and chips on the island. After making my selections, I commented on her beautiful skin and how often I had wished for a darker complexion (I'm day-glow white.) At first she was quiet, as if uncomfortable with my compliment. Then her face turned somber and she looked at me with suddenly filling eyes.

"Isn't it ironic," she said. "I look at your skin and wish mine were lighter."

Usually, I encourage new friends to share their stories. But in this instance, I decided to tell Rinda one of mine—a story my great-grandmother told me over 40 years ago, just a year before she passed away at age 96.

My great-grandmother Nora was eight years old when she met Georgia. Although they attended different schools—both in the third grade—they became instant friends, meeting after class to play in the barn behind Nora's house. Georgia's family was poor and couldn't afford to buy her much, so the two girls would often share my great-grandmother's dolls. Georgia loved playing with them and would always handle the dolls very gently, careful not to damage their porcelain faces and hand-made gowns. She told Nora that she was saving for a sewing machine and some day she would make all kinds of new dresses and hats for the dolls. Of course, Nora knew it was Georgia's mother who was saving for the machine, but it made no difference, and the two girls spent hour after hour acting out imaginary lives for the dolls.

There was nothing unusual about their friendship, except that Nora was white and Georgia was black. Both girls understood how cautious they had to be, not to let either one of their fathers see them playing together. Because they knew it would be bad—not for Nora, but for Georgia.

Late one afternoon, Nora was up in the barn loft laying out the dolls, waiting for Georgia to arrive. In a happenstance glance out the loft door, she saw someone running down the road, just beyond the cornfield. Even from that distance, she could tell it was someone small. As she watched, she said she'd "turned scared," because she could tell it was someone black, and "if one was a-running, it was because somebody was a-chasing."

As the runner got closer, Nora saw it was a little girl. About 50 yards behind, she could see a group of men—white men—quickly closing the gap, screaming curses at her, trying to catch her. In that same moment, she recognized the child's green-flowered dress.

It was Georgia!

Nora told me how her heart began to beat so hard she was sure it would explode. She stifled a cry as she watched her friend dart off the road into the cornfield and disappear between the rows, trying to hide.

Without hesitating, Nora raced from the barn and into the field, moving low through the corn stalks. When she finally got to Georgia, she found her shaking and out of breath. She told me she didn't know what else to do but put her arms around Georgia and squeeze. She said she squeezed extra hard when the group of men passed thirty feet in front of them, yelling and shouting, most of them full of the kind of courage that pours from a whisky bottle.

A few minutes later, Georgia was finally able to tell Nora what had happened. A group of white men was going house-to-house looking for a black man who thcy claimed had killed someone—someone white. That's what she'd heard them say.

Georgia said she'd never been afraid of white men before, although her daddy had told her she should be. When she saw them coming up behind her on the road, she moved to the side, to let them pass. But when they began hollering and shaking their fists at her, she ran.

It didn't matter that she was only eight. What mattered was that she was black. And running. So the men chased her.

And then for this part of the story, my great-grandmother lowered her voice to a whisper, as if she could still be punished for what she had done. Leading Georgia out of the cornfield, past the barn, and around to the back of the house, Nora pushed Georgia up and through her open bedroom window, hiding her under the bed for the rest of the day and late into the night.

At supper, Nora didn't dare tell her parents, but she did manage to sneak scraps of food from the dinner table for her friend. And later, as Nora's mother tucked her in at bedtime, she held her breath, hoping Georgia was doing the same, hiding only inches away under the mattress.

Nora waited until midnight, when she was sure her parents were asleep and it was safe for Georgia to go home. And even though it was nearly a mile away and Nora had been told never to cross the wash and go into that part of town, she and Georgia walked hand-in-hand in the dark until they were standing on the ramshackle porch of Georgia's house. Nora stayed just long enough to see her friend slip safely inside, then ran most of the way back home, sneaking in through the same window she and Georgia had used earlier, hoping her father wouldn't hear the thump of her feet when they hit the floor.

The next day, the two girls met in the barn at the usual time, but Georgia was still too shaken to play. Instead, they sat side-by-side on an old milk crate, looking out the loft door.

Nora was silent for several minutes, and then finally said, "I sometimes wish we were the same color."

"You mean white?" Georgia asked.

"It doesn't matter, just as long as we're the same. That way, we could be *real* friends, not just secret friends."

Georgia took Nora's hand and held it tight. "Then we don't have to worry, 'cause my mama says we're all the same color under God's sun."

They continued to sit, looking out the loft door until the sky was streaked with deep reds and yellows, the soft light of sunset making the difference in their skin color nearly imperceptible.

That bit of wisdom from Georgia's mother—a testament to unconditional love— also turned out to be a remarkable prediction. I met Georgia for the first time in 1971, at my great-grandmother's funeral. And although Georgia's health was poor and her hearing weak, it was still easy to see the determination and courage that had transformed a "secret" friendship into a sisterhood that had lasted for over 85 years.

As I finished my story, Rinda brought her arm up next to mine and stared down at our contrasting skin, not saying anything for the longest time. Finally, she jotted her name and phone number on a business card, inviting me to meet her for lunch that weekend, promising to take me to her favorite spot for the "best fish and chips on the island." And while she wasn't wrong about the food (admittedly great), the best part of our visit was winding up back at Orient Bay, where we spent the better part of the afternoon walking the beach hand-in-hand, trading stories about growing up—and becoming real friends under God's sun.

Life Is Too Short For Regrets

She looked tired. Her face was drawn and she'd lost weight. But she was still my Cassie, the same feisty little brunette who, at thirteen, had convinced me to steal the keys to my mother's car so we could teach each other to drive. And twenty years later, had encouraged me to give up professional photography and pursue my dream of writing. But even more important, she was one of the few girls who had stolen my heart.

I hadn't seen her in over a year, and I'd just picked her up at the airport in Ft. Lauderdale, where we would spend the weekend in the sun and surf, renewing our friendship before she left for Nassau to enjoy a week with her family.

Before checking in at our hotel, we decided to stop for dinner. As we waited in the foyer for the hostess, I wrapped my arms around Cassie and gave her a hug. From her reaction, I knew something was wrong. But before I could ask, we were on our way to the table, both of us trying to hold back the laughter as we drew obvious stares from those uncomfortable with a pair of hand-holding girlfriends.

The wine and conversation went on for hours, the two of us completely absorbed in the memories of a lifelong friendship. Eventually, our reminiscing brought us to the present, and with words no longer necessary, we settled into the moment of simply enjoying each other's company. Wanting to connect with her, to let her know how much I had missed her, I reached out and touched the side of her cheek. As she nestled into me, she closed her eyes and whispered. "I have something to tell you." I could sense she was trying to be nonchalant, but a quivering voice betrayed her. "I was diagnosed with ovarian cancer four months ago."

I sat there, unable to speak, the dinner I had just raved about threating to come up. Finally, I realized Cassie was dabbing my tears with her napkin.

"You're not allowed to cry," she protested. "I'm the privileged one here, so stop it!"

With my voice breaking, I barely got it out. "And the treatment . . . how's it going?"

Cassie shook her head. "It was too advanced."

"That's total crap! There's always something you can do."

She began stroking my hair. "And I'm doing it, by taking the next six months to squeeze everything I can from the time that's left."

"Six months?" It sounded like a death sentence, and I immediately wished I could take it back.

That's when I saw it—that familiar sense of raw spirit that had always beamed from Cassie's eyes. "Don't become one of *those people*," she warned. She drew her lips into a mock smile. "It's funny how differently some people treat me now. They think they might bruise me with the wrong words, so they talk a little slower, choosing what they say very carefully." She pulled back from me just long enough to squint her eyes. "But I expect *way* more from you."

I tried to imagine our situations reversed—what I would want from a best friend if I only had six months to finish my life. I decided right then and there to drop any pretense. Cassie deserved the *real* me, not some sympathy-driven puppet. My question came without hesitation. "Any regrets?"

Cassie nodded. "I did at first. I thought about the way I treated my parents, and the hell I put them through when I was growing up. I remembered the arguments with my stepmother, and the cruel and hateful things I said to my first husband. I wish I could change those things, and I've done my best to make amends, especially when I realized the person I had hurt the most was myself. Now I have to move on, leave the guilt and regret behind and create a life in the months I have left."

Ten minutes went by before I realized Cassie was giving me insights to leading a happier and more productive life, and I knew I'd better listen since the remainder of hers was measured in daily doses rather than years. That night, after I was sure she was asleep, I jotted down as much as I could remember.

And now, as I celebrate the anniversary of her passing, I want to share a few of those thoughts as a tribute to Cassie's legacy, remembering the impact she had on me and the others she touched as she traveled through this life.

• Realize that everyone faces adversity. And if you look, you'll easily find someone who has endured more hardship, been treated more unfairly, or been subjected to worse wrongdoing that you. Yet they've emerged from their trials and are busy living a rewarding life. We often read about people who have money, fame or power, imagining how exciting it would be to trade places with them. But for a change, try reading about someone whose situation or circumstance makes you thankful for the life you've lived.

• Let your regrets serve as lessons for the future. Rather than letting them weigh you down and prevent you from getting on with your life, resolve to learn from what happened, and to never repeat the same mistake.

• Give yourself credit for doing the best you could at the time. We all make mistakes. Based on the available information or the pressure of the situation and the circumstances, we make our decisions and hope for the best. And that's life. That's just the way things are, and beating yourself up over past choices accomplishes nothing. In fact, it's twice as punishing—you paid then and you're still paying now.

Just before Cassie boarded the plane for Nassau, she left me with one last piece of advice. It became her motto for living the rest of her very short life: Admit it, get over it, and get on with it. It's your life and it's playing out right now, with no rehearsals or timeouts. Don't waste it fretting over events and circumstances from the past. Even the difficult journeys can be an adventure.

So the next time you're feeling sorry for yourself, or consumed with bitterness, think about my Cassie, a forty-two-year-old gal who lived just long enough to leave us with a little advice, a lot of courage, and one broken heart.

The Halloween Man

In the neighborhood of my youth, Halloween was strictly for children. In small towns and rural areas, there were few, if any, Halloween parties for adults. It was simply a time for kids, costumes, and collecting candy from the neighbors. And in my eight years or so of going house-to-house in search of the cherished nugget-sized Baby Ruth or the equally prized popcorn ball, the expectation—and the result—was always the same: A smiling face, a hand extending beyond the screen door, and the reassuring plop of a piece of candy into my bag. Or in the case of old man McDougall, a ball of hard bubble gum launched at rocket speed, without any consideration to direction or specific target.

There was one man, however, who celebrated Halloween very differently. Rather than carving pumpkins or covering his house with "spooky" decorations, he found a very unique and personal way to enjoy the holiday. And while he didn't wear a costume, he did everything he could to disguise his identity.

Mr. Ardell owned a small neighborhood grocery store in Bedford Heights, Illinois. I knew him because he was the father of my best friend, Kathy. His store was close to our grammar school, and Kathy would often invite me to walk there after classes to help with her "after school job." In reality, it wasn't a job at all, and we usually spent the time hanging out together, enjoying a soda and a donut (our moms never knew), and reading all the new comic books. For a couple of twelve-year-olds, it was a lot of responsibility. At the end of the hour, we both received a quarter for our efforts.

I always enjoyed spending time in the store, and I'm sure it was because Mr. Ardell made everyone—his friends, employees, and customers—feel right at home. And although I didn't understand it at the time, there was also something special in the way that others treated *him*; they not only respected him, they knew that he was, in a truthful, honest, and reliable way—a good man. A man of integrity. The same words the preacher used to describe him at his funeral.

With the passing years, Kathy and I did our best to stay in touch, and even though we both moved away from our little hometown, we always tried to spend a couple of hours together during our visits with family over the Christmas holidays. It was during one of those visits—twenty years after the death of Mr. Ardell—that Kathy and I found ourselves reminiscing about our childhood as we enjoyed lunch at a little fast food restaurant in the older part of town. The place had been there for forty years, and neither of us had been inside since the eighth grade, when we would walk across the street from the junior high school to buy an order of fries and a Coke. There was a new counter and booths, but for the most part it looked the same, except for the pictures—old black and whites—that covered an entire wall. Old pictures of Bedford Heights. Many of them showed the downtown area from the 1930's and '40's. The original post office was there and, in later photos taken in the fifties and sixties, the J.C. Penny, the Western Auto, and the Madison Hotel coffee shop. All places I had actually been inside, shopping with my mother or in the case of the Madison Hotel, having lunch with my father.

It must have been obvious how absorbed we'd become in the old photos, as one of the women working behind the counter came over and asked Kathy if she recognized any of the old downtown area. She told her she did and, in fact, had spent much of her childhood working in her father's grocery store.

"What was the name of the store?"

Kathy told her and pointed it out in one of the pictures.

"Is your last name Ardell?"

"It used to be, before I was married."

"And the man who owned that store, he was your father?"

Although Kathy was becoming a little apprehensive at this point, she admitted it. "Yes, that was my dad."

"You wait here a minute. I'll be right back."
The woman raced back into the kitchen and
began yelling in Spanish. A burst of
conversation followed. My Spanish is terrible,
and with at least three people talking at once, I
had no idea what was going on.

In seconds the kitchen door burst open. As
the woman and her two brothers swarmed
over us, one of the men looked at Kathy and
said, "Your father would drop off groceries at
our front door. He would ring the bell and then
run back to his car!"

As we stood there, not exactly sure what
they were talking about, one of the men told us
the story. "Sometimes there was no work, and
our parents had to struggle just to put food on
the table. And they hated it, because they were
so proud, and yet they knew they needed help.
But your father, Mr. Ardell, also knew. So

they all played this game. Our parents would pretend not to know who brought the food, and your father did his best to keep it a secret, not telling anyone."

It brought a flood of memories that had never made sense until that moment.

At least once a week, just before it was time to leave the store for home, Mr. Ardell would say, "I need to fill this order and drop it off." Then he would go down the aisles, filling a large cardboard box with canned goods, soap, fresh hamburger meat, bologna, longhorn cheese, a head of lettuce, tomatoes, carrots, an onion, and a dozen potatoes. He didn't stop until the box was full, finally topping it off with a bag of penny candy and a handful of suckers.

I always wondered why he never parked close to the house where he was making the delivery. Instead, he would pull around the corner or stop several doors down, even though there was plenty of room directly in front. Leaving the engine running, he would tell Kathy and me to wait in the car while he carried the box to the door. Suddenly, he'd be running back toward us—fast. He'd jump in the seat and we'd take off.

"Just ready to go home." That's all he would say when I asked him why he always ran from each house. And now, thirty years later, I had finally discovered the truth—the real reason why he was always in a rush to get back to the car.

"We were chasing him," the woman said. "My brothers and I would hear him knocking on the screen, but when we'd open the door, there was only the box of food. The first few times, we didn't see anyone. Then later, we saw somebody running down the sidewalk. We wanted to catch him, to find out who he was. But our parents told us not to run too fast, to always let him get away. Eventually, we saw the car drive past and we knew it was the man who owned the store on the corner. Sometimes we would see both of you in the car, too. And we would think how lucky you were. To be so rich, to be able to give us candy."

To me, it was just a delivery, another order that had to be dropped off before Mr. Ardell could take me home. To the people who opened the door and found the box of food, it was kindness and compassion—and hope.

I don't believe Mr. Ardell ever told anyone what he was doing. Maybe he saw it as something that needed to be done, and he knew he was the one to do it. But even today, there are people in the small town of Bedford Heights for whom the phrase "trick-or-treat" means a great deal more than simply going door-to-door collecting candy. Instead, they treasure the memory of a man they call Mr. Halloween, a man who never wore a costume and would stealthily approach a stranger's front door in silence. And after ringing the bell, take off like a streak, determined to remain anonymous, hoping his gift would feed both body and soul—and never at the cost of another man's dignity.

A Sister's Promise

For every brother who has a little sister, there is at least one secret that she keeps. Maybe it was something she saw or heard, or a story told in confidence. Regardless of its nature, she makes a promise, often silently, never to reveal it.

I was nine when I made my first promise. My brother, Jimmy, was eleven. And it involved a most unlikely subject—a toy submarine featured for sale on the back of a cereal box.

There were lots of choices—flakes, squares, or puffs, made from corn, rice, or wheat. But the variety of grain didn't matter. The type of cereal paled in comparison to what was advertised on the back of the box. Every kid under the age of thirteen knew that's where the current offer was illustrated in blazing four-color glory. Embellished with adjectives like "incredible," "amazing," and "astonishing," the temptation was overwhelming. And yet, not all offers were the same. Of all the notable features that might prompt a young customer to buy, none was more important than the location from which the item shipped—Battle Creek, Michigan. The mere mention of that city was an unassailable testimonial, assuring the satisfaction of any pre-adolescent purchaser. It was such an important endorsement that when I overheard my brother and his friends talking about the place, I always detected a hint of reverence in their voices, as if Battle Creek were some kind of enchanted fantasyland, its lush green landscape dotted with small lakes and streams where boys sailed their boats and flew huge kites and launched rockets to the stars.

I don't remember all the promotions, just one—a working submarine. The picture on the box showed its full scale equivalent crash-diving in preparation for a decisive and heroic battle. The vivid colors and detail held my brother's attention for nearly a week. By the time he'd emptied the box of its contents, he was convinced. He had to have it.

That afternoon, I watched Jimmy use our mother's best butcher knife to cut a piece of cardboard into the same, rough shape of the envelope he would use to send his order. Carefully laying two quarters—the amount required for the purchase—in the center of the cardboard cutout, he pencil-traced around the edges of the coins, then cut out the interior circles with a smaller steak knife. After inserting the quarters and taping them flush on both sides, he explained that his efforts would prevent the dishonest interception of his cash payment, and was the only way to guarantee his new submarine would arrive on schedule (allowing four to six weeks), ready to ply the local waters of sink and tub.

A month later, the diving sub arrived in a small box about the size of a bar of soap. Jimmy nodded at the official Battle Creek postmark, satisfied that he had indeed, received the authentic article.

My brother had saved the back of the cereal box, stashing it underneath his collection of comic books. He didn't have to ask. I raced to retrieve it as he began to open the package.

When I returned, he was holding something between his fingers.

"What happened? Did a piece break off?" It was my first impression, thinking that the sub might have been damaged in the mail. But as Jimmy continued to examine the item, I could see the disappointment in his face—it wasn't *part* of the submarine, it was the entire model.

Barely two inches long, it was dull gray and fabricated with just enough intentional design to resemble a submarine. Referring to the back of the cereal box, my brother compared the details in the picture to the tiny piece of plastic. Where were the diving fins, the movable prop, the depiction of rivets, hatches, and torpedo tubes? They were certainly shown in the picture—features that he had reviewed daily, right after a visit to the mailbox to confirm the package would be at least another day in transit.

There was a small compartment on the underside of the model designed to hold a pinch of baking powder. With sub in hand, Jimmy went to the kitchen and opened the pantry. Every mom always kept a can of Clabber Girl baking powder in the pantry. But as he placed the can on the counter, he noticed the lid was loose. Would it still work? Did the clammy white powder still contain enough raw chemical energy to power the miniature boat?

I watched my brother pack the baking powder in tight and push on the cap. It only took a moment to decide the route for the sub's maiden voyage—a short run across the bathroom sink. He rested the tiny boat in his open hand and slowly lowered it into the water. It sank to the bottom. Then slowly, it began to pitch forward. Lifting off the porcelain, the little piece of plastic rose to the top of the water, broke the surface and immediately rolled on its side, releasing a single bubble. Returning to the bottom of the sink, it repeated the process a half dozen times until the baking powder was exhausted.

My brother didn't display his new sub with his other models. It was too tiny, too vague in appearance. More important, I knew he wanted to avoid the embarrassment of an awkward explanation when his friends asked the inevitable question, "What is it?" For weeks he had promised they would share in the excitement of watching it dive through the water as a stream of bubbles poured off its chemical engine (just like on the back of the cereal box). Once, I heard him comment that he might have to find a larger body of water— that to demonstrate the sub's speed and full maneuvering capabilities could easily require a backyard pool.

His friends forgot about the sub. But I don't think my bother did–not for a long time. I'm sure it was his first real disappointment over something he purchased with his own money. Later on he would learn the meaning of the phrase, "actual product may differ from illustration," just as he would also learn that reality often turns out to be a far cry from expectations.

From that day on, I never mentioned the submarine. Not to my brother, and certainly never to his friends. Perhaps I intuitively knew that before long, I would be facing my own embarrassing disappointments and, instead of a self-righteous lecture, I would need my big brother's support and understanding.

About a month after it arrived, I saw Jimmy pitch the toy into the trash. He had kept it hidden in one of his dresser drawers and, while looking for a t-shirt, had decided he no longer wanted to be reminded of how gullible he'd been. After I was sure he had left the house, I retrieved it and tucked it away inside my ballerina jewelry box. The box has been gone for years, but I still have the little sub. It's one of my most prized possessions, reminding me that the bond between brothers and sisters is often forged by the realization that a regret or two is easier to handle if it's shared, sometimes with a promise of silence.

Living Life in the First Person

It's really amazing how much can change—especially for the better—in a single year. I've moved to Florida, downsized my living space and, in general, made changes intended to simplify my life.

It was time. After residing in the same state for thirty years, I was ready to leave my no-longer-rewarding accumulations of predictability and repetition. I wanted the opportunity to explore new places and meet new people while experiencing—and appreciating—the influence of a different regional history and culture.

Anxious to investigate my new surroundings, I reveled in "first-time discoveries." From savoring the flavor of local dishes to learning that Southern hospitality often takes the form of easy conversation with a stranger—without expectation or agenda—it prompted me to think about the relationship between a life well-lived and one full of new experiences. Obviously, our days can't always be filled with an endless stream of spontaneous exploration and pleasant surprises. But without an adventurous spirit and a willingness to try new things, we can easily lose our zest for life, trading possibility for the illusion of security.

The idea of living a life full of "firsts" prompted me to ask my husband which of his experiences were the most significant—those special times and moments that had truly made his life richer and more complete.

His answer included the expected highlights of our relationship: our first date, the first night we spent together, and our first out-of-town trip. As he thought about earlier events—before we met—he remembered his first day of school, his first two-wheel bike, and the last Christmas he spent with his dad. He was quiet for a moment, and then without any explanation, disappeared into his office. He returned with a stack of old letters and what looked like birthday cards. After sifting through the pile, he pulled out one of the letters and set it in front of me.

Then he told me about his Aunt Katie—the "First Lady" of his family.

Born in 1903, she experienced some very difficult times. Her older brother was killed in WWI. She lost her husband in WWII. Her only daughter passed away at age 40. Aunt Katie had cancer—and survived. Her life was one of sacrifice, sorrow, and hardship. But you would never know it. Always happy and positive, she made everyone feel better just because she was in the room. If there was a piano in the house, she was pounding away on it, singing at the top of her lungs. And while she wasn't particularly talented, educated, or accomplished—at least not by traditional standards—her grandkids, nephews, nieces, friends, and acquaintances all sought her advice and counsel. And she always had time to listen. To those who knew her, she was truly a "First Lady" in every sense of the term.

Although Aunt Katie is no longer with us (she passed away three years ago at the age of 104), she left a special kind of legacy in the form of a letter written to my husband on his 21st birthday. On two hand-written pages, she revealed her "secrets" to life—not just how to live it, but how to savor it, how to squeeze every last drop of juice from it. In her words, it was a recipe for living life in the first person. And so, with my husband's permission, here are Aunt Katie's seven keys to a life well-lived.

- *Decide what you want from life and take the risk.* Although you may experience failure along the way, you'll never have to wonder about how things might have been. Remember that a life that simply passes is a life that is wasted. Life is meant to be lived. See it. Travel through it. Experience it. Leave your mark on it.

- *Be authentic.* Pretending to be someone different than who you really are is exhausting—and deceiving. How will you know if others truly like and respect the "real" you if you wear a false personality and engage in activities that you don't enjoy?

- *Life will meet your expectations, whether good or bad.* Worrying about things is the fastest way to go to the hospital.

- *Telling someone that they can do better isn't always true.* They may be doing the very best they can at that point in their life. Instead, offer to help.

- *Happiness is a "do."* When I feel down, I go outside and work in the garden or find something to keep me occupied in the kitchen. I'll often bake something for a neighbor. And after a while, I know I'm going to be okay. The world is full of bad things—war, hate, injustice. But in my little corner of it—the place I make for myself and others—it's always a good place, just as good as I know how to make it. And with enough good places, the bad ones will lose ground and eventually disappear.

- *Don't try to think for others or try to assume their grief or take over their worries.* You were made to handle your own life, and each person gets their share, their own burdens to bear. Sometimes I need a helping hand, other times I give one. But at the end of the day, I'm the only one responsible for how I feel about what happens to me. And that goes for both the good and the bad.

- *Do the best you can—when you can—then let it go.* Feeling guilty is a double loss. You wind up being upset about the past, which means you're not at your best to handle the present. Just remember, guilt is your mind's way of telling you that you can do better. Learn the lesson, then turn the page and move on.

Because of distance and circumstances, my visits with Aunt Katie were far too infrequent.

But her letter, written thirty-five years ago, confirms what I had always suspected—that she lived a life full of meaning and purpose, and without any doubt, a life full of "firsts."

Packed With a Promise

On Veterans Day, we honor and commemorate the men and women who have served our country through their military service. Our focus is naturally directed toward those who fought our country's enemies, unselfishly risking their lives to preserve a way of life that is without equal anywhere in the world. Most of these men and women have very personal stories about their war-time duty—memories about a particular event or situation that touched their lives while, in many cases, they were far from home.

In the latter part of 2010, I was privileged to learn about one of those memories from an eighty-six-year-old woman named Betty. Occupying the room next to my aunt in an assisted care facility located just outside Phoenix, Betty suffered from early onset Alzheimer's, yet she always appeared bright and lucid, especially when sharing the latest accomplishments of her four great-grandchildren. Stopping in to see Betty after spending time with my aunt had become a regular part of my visit, and it was during one of our chats that Betty showed me a letter she'd received in 1943 from an Army Air Force Staff Sergeant stationed in Alconbury, England. It was a very unusual letter, especially since Tommy Banning had never met Betty.

During WWII, Betty worked as a parachute packer or "chute rigger." She knew the dire circumstances that many of the men faced when they were forced to bail out of disabled aircraft, so she had developed the practice of slipping a tiny note under one of the outside flaps of the chute-bag in the hope of lifting the spirits of the soldiers who wore them. She wrote the notes at home before her shift and took them to work with her. Although Betty composed different messages, this is the one she most frequently penned: *"I hope you never have to use this, but if you do, don't worry, I took extra care in packing it - Betty"*

She had been "personalizing" her work for about four months when one of her notes received the following reply:

Dear Betty,

My name is Tommy Banning and I'm twenty years old (or will be on October 14). I'm a turret gunner on a B-17 and I'm stationed at Alconbury, England. I found out there are two places our company's chutes are packed. Since I only know your first name, I'm writing to both places on the chance this letter will find you. I found your note inside my chute and after reading it, I put it in my pocket. At the time, I didn't know why. Now I do.

Two weeks ago we were flying a mission over Regensburg, Germany. At first nobody thought the hit was serious. We're hit with flack all the time. And just like always we kept flying through it. But after another minute or so we started to lose altitude. Three shorts on the alarm told us to get our chutes on. Then the captain told us the outboard engines were gone and the hydraulics were shot up. He was going to try to hold the plane level as long as possible but it wasn't long before we were more nose down than level. I don't remember hearing the order to bail out. It just seemed like we were all moving toward our assigned hatch. I don't think any of us really thought about what we were doing, we just did it the way we'd been taught.

The air blast was hard, like hitting a wall. And then for the first time I was scared. There hadn't been time to think about it before but now I was falling. I got a glimpse of the plane once but then it was just blurred sky and clouds and the ground and the sound of the air rushing by me. And then I heard the pop and felt the jerk that brought me right side up. I looked up and saw white. Below me the ground was where it should be.

There were ten of us on the plane. Six of us found each other on the ground right away. I can't tell you where we were when we went down but we stayed together until a resistance unit picked us up the following day. The other four men are still missing.

I know the work must be backbreaking. Standing on your feet all day, carefully folding to make sure nothing gets tangled. So I thought you should know that every time I look at a chute I think about you. Even though I've never met you or have any idea what you look like, I think about you. Because the chute you packed saved my life that day.

Like I said, I found your note inside my chute that morning and shoved it in my pocket. And at the time, I didn't know why I kept it. Now I do.

I've included my address so you can write and tell me if this letter gets to you. It would mean a lot to me.

"Did you answer him?" I asked.

Betty nodded. "I did. I sent him a birthday card."

Being a romantic at heart, I immediately pursued the possibilities. "So did you correspond back and forth? Did you have a chance to meet him after the war?"

Betty reached out and took the letter, skimming over the faded ink with her arthritic-plagued fingers, doing her best to fold it and place it back in the envelope. "It was a month or so before I received another letter," she said. "It came from some captain or group leader—I forget which. He said his crew had celebrated Tommy's birthday early in the morning over breakfast. The men had raised their coffee cups in a toast. It was all they had time for."

"Did you ever hear from him again?" I asked.

"No, dear. Never again."

I could see how tired she was, so I said my goodbyes and left.

Five months later, Betty was gone.

It took over six months of researching archives and surviving veterans groups to piece together the rest of Tommy's story. And through the gracious cooperation of Betty's family, I was eventually able to get a copy of Tommy's letter.

Here's what I learned: There was a reason Betty never heard from Tommy again—one that she had either forgotten or simply didn't want to talk about. On October 14, 1943, a force of two hundred ninety-one B-17's attacked the ball-bearing works at Schweinfurt, Germany. The planes were met by over three hundred German fighter aircraft. The ensuing battle resulted in the loss of sixty B-17's shot down over Germany, and five more crashing short of the runway as they attempted to land in England. Over six hundred men did not return from that mission. Tommy was one of them. On his twentieth birthday, Tommy's plane was hit by rocket fire. It exploded over the skies of Germany, killing all on board.

The group leader had written to Betty because of how much her birthday card had meant to Tommy. It had been found inside the lid of his storage chest when his personal items were removed from the crew quarters. Since both of Tommy's parents were deceased and he had no siblings, it was the only card he had received.

While it's difficult to imagine what Tommy experienced that day, I like to think he took a moment to read Betty's card just one more time before he left for the airfield, happy that he had made a new friend, someone who cared enough about him to remember his twentieth birthday. Maybe he was thinking about her as he took his position behind the ball turret's machine gun, even considering the possibility that Betty might turn out to be much more than just a "pen-pal."

This I know for sure: Nearly seventy years later, a woman named Betty still kept his letter as one of her most cherished possessions. To her, it was part of Tommy's legacy—a roughly written note of appreciation, thanking her for her tireless efforts that had saved his life on an August day in 1943.

What Might Have Been

My twenty-fifth high school reunion was just two weeks away. I should have been excited—but I wasn't. With the deadline for my column looming at the end of the week, and the final round of editing for my next book staring me in the face, flying back to my hometown to reminisce with nearly-forgotten friends, locker buddies, and study hall partners was not high on my list of priorities. But I also knew there was a part of me—a volley-ball-whacking, Coke-and-fries-eating, rock-and-roll-loving teen—that would be disappointed if I didn't go. Hoping to sway my responsible reluctance with a dose of nostalgia, I pulled out my senior yearbook and read a few scribbled ramblings from my old classmates—

platitudes and clichés that have personalized every high school yearbook since the marriage of ballpoint pen to glossy paper. *"Best of luck in the future." "See you in college. Hope you'll let me copy your homework." "Enjoyed our chats in math class."*

I was able to recall most of the names, but there was one entry from a boy I couldn't place. "Wish we had spent more time together," he wrote. A bit more heart-felt than most, but not enough to jog my memory.

I put the book away and went back to work. I didn't think any more about the comment until two weeks later, when I came face-to-face with its author.

The reunion party was earmarked by all the usual characteristics: a rented banquet hall, some hastily prepared table decorations, and a few balloons taped over doorways. As I made my way to the reception table, it was impossible to ignore the unmistakable uncertainty in the air. The electric charge of youthful anticipation ever-so-present at seventeen had been replaced by awkward pauses and quick scans at nametags, making it clear how time had affected our memories—and expectations.

As I ate my wilted salad and pretended to enjoy the overdone roast beef, I reminisced with girlfriends about hairstyles, prom nights, the teachers we liked, and of course, some of the boys we dated. As we picked at the dessert—dry chocolate cake—prizes were awarded for the person who had traveled the farthest, changed the most, and been married the longest. One of the gals at the table wondered out loud if the emcee was the same overly aggressive twerp who hadn't been able to keep his hands off the typing instructor.

As we began to run out of small talk, it became obvious that four years of high school was, in most cases, our only commonality, and a few adolescent memories could not compete with the twenty-five years of life that had passed since. As the conversation turned to career concerns, aging parents, and unappreciative offspring, I found myself drifting away from the group. Retreating to an outside patio, I sat at an empty table to collect my thoughts. I had been there less than a minute when I was approached by someone I didn't recognize.

"Hi, Jaye, I was hoping you'd be here."

I couldn't place him. He was definitely familiar, but I couldn't make the connection. I managed a few clumsy questions about mutual friends and teachers, yet I was still clueless. Then he asked if I had kept the old Chevy Nova I drove in my senior year. I felt terrible. He had recognized me, even remembering the car I used to drive. I finally had to admit it—I didn't remember him.

"That's okay," he said. "It's my fault for not wearing my nametag. I'm Neil Graham. My locker was across the hall from yours. We were also in senior English together."

The memories came rushing back. In high school, he'd been an anomaly—good looking, athletic, smart—and painfully quiet. Seldom seen at school dances or other social functions, he didn't seem to have a lot of friends, and yet he usually offered a smile to anyone passing by, as if silently inviting them to stop and chat.

As we became reacquainted, our conversation flowed relaxed and easy. He reminded me about the Spring Fever dance in the cafeteria, when Michael Sanders drenched my new pink taffeta dress with Coke. He confessed to sitting behind me in the theater on a rainy Saturday afternoon during our junior year—I didn't know it—to watch "Poltergeist."

I learned that he'd been married for eight years, had a family, and loved to sail. He told me he'd majored in marine biology in college, and after graduation had moved to the west coast to work at one of the research institutes. Taking advantage of the first lull in the conversation, he pushed back his chair and stood.

"I'll be right back," he promised. "There's someone I want you to meet."

He returned a few minutes later with his wife. She shook my hand, and the three of us exchanged small talk until she excused herself to go inside and retrieve her sweater.

And then he said it . . .

"You know, I had a huge crush on you all through high school. But I was just too shy to ask you out. Night after night, I picked up the phone and dialed all the numbers except the last one. I guess I was afraid to let it ring, knowing you might answer and then I wouldn't know what to say."

As he told me about those nights from so many years ago, he admitted that he'd even written out a complete script with different responses based on how I might answer his questions. We laughed as he readily admitted how silly he had been, allowing his lack of experience and risk of rejection to keep him from having a simple phone conversation.

"I kept hoping we'd bump into each other in the hallway," he continued, "or we'd wind up sitting together in one of those break-out sessions we used to have in English class. But it never happened. And even years later, I still tried to imagine what my life would have been like, if I'd only had a little more courage."

I told him how flattered I was, and that indeed, I wished he'd been a bit more bold, assuring him that I would have accepted his invitation.

An hour later we were saying our goodbyes. And in one of those brief, yet never-to-be-forgotten moments, while his wife was busy exchanging business cards with a new acquaintance, Neil left me with a bittersweet tribute to all the secret loves that remain unspoken.

"I've always wondered how much different my life would have been with you in it," he said. And without hesitating, he added, "And even today, I still do."

Wanting to say more but knowing I couldn't, I told him how nice it was to see him again, and how much I enjoyed meeting his wife. It was all I could think of.

True to tradition, we exchanged our yearbooks and updated our original comments. Finally, he thanked me for spending the time to reminisce with him and then mentioned something about his babysitting mom expecting them home by midnight. And with that, the night became another memory.

On the drive home I stopped for coffee and, on a whim, took my high school annual inside the restaurant to look at the new comments I'd gathered at the reunion. I turned directly to Neil's picture, curious about what he had added to his original note.

"If I had only known what was waiting for me, I would have taken the chance," he wrote. And then he signed it, "Silwy."

The signature didn't make any sense—at least not to me—until two months later, when my niece asked if she could look through the old annual. The unusual signature brought her running, with the translation: *Still in love with you.*

For days, it was all I could think about—how he must have felt, keeping his feelings a secret, especially from me, a girl who had spent more than her share of Saturday nights in front of the TV set while others always seemed to have dates. And frankly, I felt a little cheated, wondering how many guys never understood I was simply waiting to be asked.

That night—that experience—had a huge impact on me. It inspired *The Possibilities of Amy*. It also made me realize how many opportunities life offers us—especially in our youth. But because we're afraid of rejection or lack confidence, we decide to let possibility pass us by, not realizing how one simple action can often lead to a completely different outcome in life.

Finally, it left me with a nagging uncertainty that has surely haunted every adult who takes a moment to look back at life from the perspective of hindsight: *What would I have done differently if I knew then what I know now?*

The Angels of Ellis Island

For most of us, Thanksgiving is typically a time to reunite with family and gain a few pounds from over-enjoying a table loaded with the requisite turkey, dressing, and all the trimmings. The day is also a highlight for football fans as well as signaling the traditional start of seasonal parties and marathon shopping sprees.

It's quite a contrast from the holiday's earliest beginnings when, in 1621, the Pilgrims of New England celebrated a day of thanksgiving in gratitude for their good health and harvest, prompted in part by the death of half of the Plymouth colony from starvation and cold during the previous winter.

Even in our country's more recent history, there are examples of Thanksgiving representing more than just the start of the frenzied holiday season—when it signified a defining touchstone in life, an inspirational reminder about those who overcame personal adversity and difficult challenges, and were grateful to have survived.

I recently spent some time with a new friend who considers the Thanksgiving of 1907 as one of those historical milestones still celebrated by her family. That year, President Theodore Roosevelt signed a special proclamation urging Americans to observe the day with prayer, his request even more significant because it also marked a year when over a million immigrants passed through the Great Hall at Ellis Island—a time when people from all parts of Europe came looking for a better life and a new beginning in a strange and wonderful country called America.

One of those immigrants was a woman named Molly. From her family records, I learned that Molly was a slight woman and about 30 years of age at the time she made the crossing. She had lost her husband to cholera three years prior and, as a widow, she knew the transition to a new life in another country would be difficult. She would have to leave everything behind, sail across the ocean to an unfamiliar city without the promise of a job, a place to stay, or a single friend to help her get settled. And she would have to do it with her seven-year-old son, William.

For over two years, she had saved her money—enough to buy third class passage on a steamship. And right up until the day of sailing, her friends tried to talk her out of leaving. "Even the voyage itself will be a challenge," they told her. Third class passengers (called steerage) were restricted to the bottom decks, where they often spent the majority of the two-week Atlantic crossing in their bunks, seasick and restricted from the open decks and fresh air.

But Molly was determined. She wanted to raise William where he would have the opportunity to obtain the education she never received, and to achieve financial independence equal to his efforts. She wasn't making the trip for herself. She was making the change—the sacrifice—for her son.

Like the rest of the steerage passengers, Molly and William boarded the ship and settled into the cramped public accommodations. They shared six bathrooms with eight hundred other people and waited in long lines for a meal of soup and stale bread—with Molly always keeping a watchful eye on William. At night, she told him stories about the school he would attend, about the new friends he would soon have, and about all the wonderful things they would see and do together in a magical city called New York.

She planned to find work in the garment district. She had been told that laundries and tailors were the best options for immigrants, and with her sewing skills, she hoped to find a job that paid well enough to afford a one bedroom flat in a boarding house on the lower west side. It was where the poor eked out a living, but it was a start. And that was all Molly wanted—a chance to provide a better life for her son.

Molly's dreams of opportunity and success for William kept her motivated and focused during the difficult trip. However, the future she planned for William was one she would never see. On the sixth day of the crossing, Molly complained of headaches and dizziness. Three days later, she was dead.

It's difficult to imagine the loneliness—the fear—that seven-year-old William was forced to endure. With no family or friends, he found himself abandoned and helpless. During my conversation with his granddaughter, she described it best: "It had to be hell on earth." Reserved, in this instance, for the innocent.

Unfortunately, William's situation was not the exception. Every year, thousands of orphans were shuttled from Ellis Island to waiting jails, almshouses, and orphanages to suffer an unimaginable childhood. Even as bad as those choices were, the alternatives were worse—living in the slums, on the street, or being turned over to the Children's Aid Society to be shipped west on the controversial Orphan Train, where both boys and girls were indentured to host families who needed able-bodied laborers, regardless of age.

It was a far cry from the dreams that Molly had held for her son. But it was William's probable future.

Upon arrival at Ellis Island, William was herded off the ship and moved into the Great Hall. After a quick examination to confirm the absence of cholera or tuberculosis symptoms, he was transferred to the mainland terminal by ferry. Once inside, he was taken to a small room, its only window looking into a dimly lit hallway. Volunteers from the children's mission usually made their pick-ups in the late afternoon, just in time for William to receive a late supper and a bed assignment.

An hour later, William had traded the hard chairs for a place on the floor. Too scared to sleep, but too tired to keep his eyes open, he eventually dozed off, only to be awakened by the surprise of a hand lightly covering his. He looked up to see a young couple bending over him.

"My name is Betsy and this is my husband, Benjamin. What's your name?"

William managed to whisper it before making his way to his feet.

"I'm going to make dinner in a few hours and I know you must be hungry. Would you like to come home with us?"

William barely nodded, but for Betsy and Ben Hansen, it was enough. A few minutes later, they were helping him into Ben's supply wagon, making sure he saw the small bag of clothing they had retrieved from the

140

terminal—the clothes Molly had packed for her son.

Betsy and Ben had found William just minutes before the missionaries arrived. Ben was in the terminal to make a delivery of steam-pipe to one of the ships docked in New York harbor. On that particular day, Betsy had decided to tag along, to have the rare treat of enjoying lunch with her husband. Married for eight years, they lived above the pipe-fitters shop that employed Ben.

Betsy and Ben had never considered themselves to be potential adoptive parents, and they certainly weren't actively looking for a new addition to their family. They were already the proud parents of two girls, Sarah and Opal. But it didn't matter. They made their decision spontaneously, without planning or concern for the additional burden another child would bring to their already tenuous economic situation, or the effect a new sibling might have on their daughters. They simply knew they couldn't leave William in that room by himself.

That evening, William sat between his new sisters and ate his first Thanksgiving dinner in America. And although the menu was quite different from the traditional fare we enjoy today—a chicken took the place of turkey, and each family member enjoyed half a sweet potato—the table was overflowing with unconditional acceptance. Later that night, William slept on a small couch in the living room. But even in his fragile and confused state of mind, he somehow knew he was safe.

It was nearly a year before William made it through an entire day without missing his mother. And it was on that very same day that he called Betsy, *mom*. It happened while he was headed out the door on his way to school. Betsy waited until she was sure William was completely down the stairs before she let go of the tears she had been holding back for over ten months. Finally, she knew—William was part of the family.

Ben and Betsy Hansen raised two beautiful daughters and one fine son. A son who fought in WWI and was awarded the Citation Star for gallantry in action. A son who married his high school sweetheart and had three children of his own. A son who never forgot his first Thanksgiving in America, when one of the angels of Ellis Island reached down to take his hand and bring him home.

According to the national immigration records, over 50,000 orphaned children were received at Ellis Island. It's unknown how many were "unofficially" adopted, but some estimates put the number at only six to eight percent. There were no lengthy forms to fill out or minimum requirements to meet. Most adoptions were as simple as William's, done by extending an open hand, literally offering the gift of life to a frightened and lonely child.

So this year, as you gather around the table with your family and friends, be thankful for the blessings and fortunate happenstances that give your life meaning and substance. And then offer a special thanks to the thousands of people who, just like Ben and Betsy, perform miraculous acts of kindness and compassion every day, surely earning themselves a place with the angels.

Middle-Age Crazy

I received a lot of feedback and comments following the release of *The Possibilities of Amy,* including some revealing emails filled with poignant and bittersweet stories about high school romances that didn't happen. It seems taking a hind-sighted look at our adolescence produces as much frustration as nostalgia. But we were young and naïve (some of us, anyway) and our old friends, reason and logic, were often overwhelmed by our hormone-charged emotions.

Not all the emails, however, were focused on the teen years. One person wrote, *"Sometimes, when I think about my twenties, I'm certain I would have been better off if I'd put my life-clock on hold and skipped the decade entirely."*

Another summed up her twenties in two words: *"surprise and disappointment."*

Their comments stirred my own memories from those ten years. I found the usual imprints collected by most young people rushing through their twenties: a first marriage, the shockwaves of divorce, the strange sense of frustration and helplessness over death, and the guilt that rises from goodbyes that were never meant to be permanent. In short, it was very different from the magical whirlwind of optimism and opportunity portrayed by a media-inspired youth culture and its not-so-subtle suggestion that a fresh, unlined face was a first class ticket to new adventures and assured success.

Maybe that's the problem. For most of us, the reality of our young-adult years was a far cry from the never-ending peak experience we believed it was going to be. Our generation had expectations beyond those of the previous—or any generation since. We wanted the *right* occupation—one that would provide an outlet for personal expression and the opportunity to make a unique and lasting impact on the world. Determined our personal life not separate from the professional, we promised ourselves they would flow together, blending in a synergistic ooze of Peter Max graphics and Desiderata posters. When it came to relationships, we insisted our chosen mate have just the right amount of yin to balance our yang. And if we experienced one of our periodic but certain sexual lows, we told ourselves we could top off our tanks with an occasional sniff from the flower garden growing across the street or next door, depending on who was home.

Instead of distracting our minds with an iPod, we filled our brains with concepts, visualizing our lives as an expandable space in which we could create a compelling destiny— EST bubbles, inflated with honest intention and designed to accommodate our finest moments. But for reasons that still escape us, they were never occupied. Why do we have all these vacancies?

I think we overbuilt.

So now, twenty years later, we join the gym, cut back on the desserts, and hope our friends notice how much younger we look. And yet there is a nagging thought that persistently haunts our efforts: Even if we were able to force our bodies into double overtime and score just one dream performance, it would be out of sequence, a belated consolation for what might have been. It is an inescapable paradox of life, and the irony couldn't be more clear—the difference between making it real and compensating for reality continues to be driven apart by the wedge of time.

Which brings us to the big question: Now what?

Are we resigned to face each other in yoga classes and ponder the strength of those invisible threads that connect us—to each other, to the big picture, to monkeys on an island whose name we can't pronounce? Or do we take a less physically-demanding approach, and start shopping for a comfy overstuffed rocker so we can while away the days trying to remember that exact moment when circumstances scrubbed our chance to be an original in a world choking with boring predictability and repetition?

All very heady stuff—but not very

productive.

Life is far too short—and precious—to waste. Spending what's left of it in a state of constant introspection can be costly, especially as we get older and time becomes more valuable, and we have more to be introspective about. (Get the insanity of it all?)

Perhaps the key to dealing with the past is to value the perspective it can bring to the future. Hidden in our angst, there is purpose and, even more important, promise. Our bittersweet memories of lost love, fortune, and prosperity can become gentle reminders that life is simply what we choose to make it. The best we can do is periodically examine our lives, check our direction, and make adjustments. Maybe that's been the plan all along—to spend the first thirty-five years or so getting acquainted with ourselves. And then listen to the feedback from our souls. The fact that we feel a bit of disappointment—even frustration—are all signs of a working receiver.

I'll leave you with this: There is something very liberating about facing the demons of our youth. It instills a greater appreciation for the "now," giving us the courage to move forward with not only a calm acceptance of the past, but also an optimistic resolve for the future.

Maybe good ol' Forrest Gump had it right all along—except in my case, life is just a box of Good & Plenty.

A Gift From the Mayans

According to the Mayan calendar, the current 5125 year-long cycle will end on December 21, 2012. The idea has made for some interesting movies and several best-selling books—most of which are little more than over-dramatized fiction with little basis in fact.

There is, however, a small group of people who have construed this event to be the literal end of time—and life—on this planet. Other radical interpretations suggest the "end-of-days calendar" is really a kind of astronomic timetable, warning us of apocalyptic changes in weather and geo-centricity that could result in the loss of much of the world's infrastructure that we now take for granted.

The world's leading experts have assured us that we have little to fear. And that in all likelihood, December 21 will come and go without incident, with most people's thoughts focused on Christmas shopping, holiday parties, and eggnog.

Seems like a shame, really, to have an ancient civilization like the Mayans—who left us with such a nifty collection of temples and the basis for modern day astronomy—predict such a significant event without attributing *some* credibility to their efforts.

Maybe our mistake in considering the 2012 prediction is our "all or nothing" context. By thinking only in terms of extreme opposites— catastrophic prophecy or entirely meaningless timekeeping—we might be overlooking a more fertile middle-ground.

Just for fun, let's consider the re-setting of the Mayan calendar with a different mentality. What if, rather than predicting a cataclysmic end to our way of life, the Mayans were encouraging future generations to periodically examine their lives, re-evaluate their priorities and, if necessary, make a few changes?

Personally, I like the idea. And it started me thinking: What if, for the next few months, I decided to live my life as if the world really *was* coming to an end? How would I spend my time? Where would I go? Who would I want to see—and what would we talk about—if I knew it would be my last conversation with that person?

I quickly realized it would put a different perspective on the way I use my time—a different set of rules to live by. Now I was hooked. I decided to determine what my *New*

Rules would be, considering them as little reminders to keep me focused on the things in life that were important. If you find any of them useful, feel free to borrow, modify, or adapt to your own situation—not only for the balance of this year, but for all the years to come.

- **Go your own way.** Live life by *your* standards. If you decide to adopt other people's lifestyles, dictates, and doctrines, do so only if it's right for you. Once we've reached adulthood, we've earned the right to call our own shots—to live where we choose, see who we want, and to spend our time in ways that are personally satisfying. As long as our choices don't hurt others, we have the right to explore the opportunities of a lifetime.

- **Use every day to advantage**. Recognize that the days are passing. Our time is limited, so make each day count for something. When we're twenty, the future is a vague and seemingly endless string of tomorrows. But those with the majority of their years behind them often encourage us to spend our time consciously, and in ways that make us—and others—happy. One of my closest family friends (now eighty-six) put it extremely well: *"Don't celebrate your eightieth birthday still wishing you had traveled more, worried less, made more friends, visited family more often, repaired broken relationships, or been more willing to try new things."* Whether you are looking at another fifty years or another five, live every day in appreciation of how you spend your time.

• **Remain flexible to change.** Remember, life is what happens while you're planning your future. It seldom works out the way we think it will. But it does work out. Being receptive to alternative experiences can be a real source of joy and excitement.

- **Regardless of what happens, don't take it too seriously.** Socrates suggested it. Shakespeare said it. And Will Rogers made it a classic. Most recently, it was repeated very eloquently by Bill Harris, a brain-wave researcher and founder of the Centerpointe Research Institute: *"We adopt the role of actor, witness, or author, giving our hearts fully to the game of life, knowing all the while that it is a great diversion and will eventually end."*

Personally, I'm looking forward to living life to its fullest on December 21st, and in all the days that follow.

If you enjoyed this book, I hope you'll tell your friends and write a review on the Amazon book page at:

LoveTravelsForever.com

About the Author

Jaye Frances is the author of seven books including *The New Girl in Town* and the suspense thriller trilogy, *World Without Love*. Her other published works include *The Beach*, *The Kure*, and *Love Travels Forever*. Storyteller, truth-seeker, and optimist, Jaye explores relationships, philosophy, and the complexities of life—a day at a time.

For more info, visit:

JayeFrances.com
JayeFrancesBooks.com
JayeFrancesYouTube.com
JayeFrances.Substack.com
LinkedIn.com/in/JayeFrances
Facebook.com/JayeFrancesAuthor
Twitter.com/JayeFrancesNews

Books by Jaye Frances
World Without Love Series

Betrayed
Book One - World Without Love

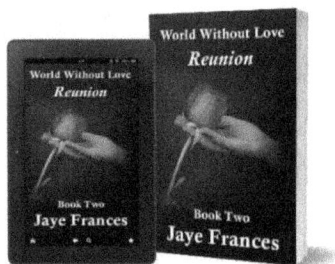

Reunion
Book Two - World Without Love

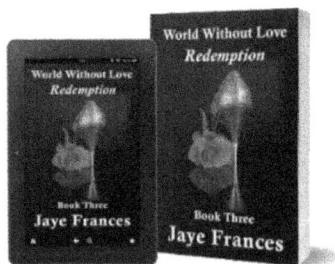

Redemption
Book Three - World Without Love

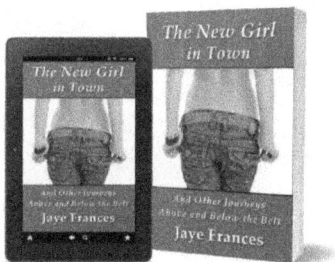

The New Girl in Town
And Other Journeys Above and Below the Belt

The Beach
Including the Novella, Short Time

The Kure

Love Travels Forever

Jaye Frances Books are Available in eBook
and Paperback at JayeFrancesBooks.com

World Without Love - The Series
Betrayed – Reunion - Redemption
Betrayed
Book One - *World Without Love*

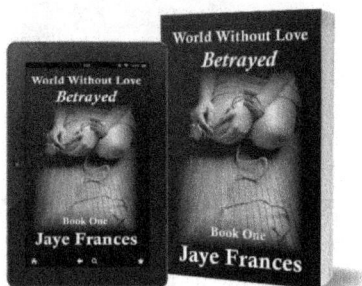

Jewel has everything going for her—a handsome husband, a promising future, and lots of time to explore an island paradise she now calls home. But when a group of strangers accompanies her husband home for a friendly game of poker, her life quickly becomes a hellish nightmare of deceit and betrayal.

Now her very survival depends on entering a world where sex, domination, and money are inseparable, where women must obey all masters, and where every desire has its price.

World Without Love contains mature content and is intended for an 18+ audience

Betrayed is available in eBook and paperback at
BetrayedBookOne.com

Reunion
Book Two - *World Without Love*

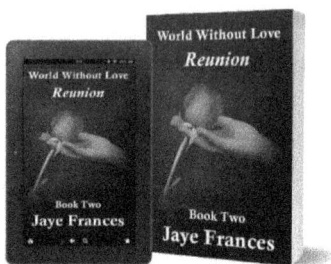

In **Reunion**, Jewel's story continues as she finds herself stranded in a far-flung corner of the world. Struggling to elude her captors and a network of bounty hunters, she meets her would-be savior, a man who promises to provide protection and comfort. Believing her nightmare has finally come to an end, Jewel begins making plans to return home, where she can start her life over again.

But greed raises its ugly head, and the terrifying future she thought she'd evaded becomes a reality. Deceived by the only one she believed she could trust, Jewel is left defenseless against the sadistic abusers who take pleasure in teaching her their own form of discipline. With the dream of rescue and returning home to San Diego even further from her reach, she begins planning her revenge on the men who have stolen her life—and her future.

World Without Love contains mature content and is intended for an 18+ audience.

Reunion is available eBook and paperback at
ReunionBookTwo.com

Redemption
Book Three - *World Without Love*

Rescued from Bangkok's evil flesh markets, Jewel's victory over her captors is bittersweet. Haunted by her last memories of Annie, Jewel vows to do whatever it takes to find her friend—hopefully in time to save her from a sadistic killer. Using her new position as an embassy hostess, Jewel begins to form alliances with the constant stream of visiting political attaches and power brokers, hoping one of them can help find Annie—still alive.

Quick to recognize Jewel's special assets, her supervisors offer her more responsibility, and with it, the benefits of unsupervised travel and the latitude to call her own shots in the completion of her duties. No longer under the scrutiny of the all-seeing covert government network, Jewel realizes she has been given another special privilege, one that her superiors could not have anticipated—the freedom to extract revenge on all those who attempted to destroy her life.

But again, the hand fate touches Jewel's heart. And before she can stop herself, a professional relationship becomes very personal, forcing her to choose between the man she loves and the one who helped her escape a dismal world of enslavement and cruel domination.

World Without Love contains mature content
and is intended for an 18+ audience

Redemption is available in eBook and paperback at
RedemptionBookThree.com

World Without Love – **The Complete Series**
Includes ***Betrayed, Reunion, and Redemption***

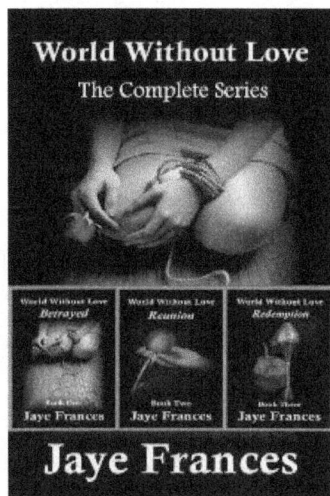

In ***Betrayed***, Jewel has everything going for her—a handsome husband, a promising future, and lots of time to explore an island paradise she now calls home. But when a group of strangers accompanies her husband home for a friendly game of poker, her life quickly becomes a hellish nightmare of deceit and betrayal. Now her very survival depends on entering a world where sex, domination, and money are inseparable, where women must obey all masters, and where every desire has its price.

Jewel's story continues in ***Reunion***, as she finds herself alone and stranded in a far-flung corner of the world. Struggling to elude her captors and the network of bounty hunters, she meets her would be savior, a man who promises to provide protection and comfort. Jewel believes her nightmare has finally come to an end. But greed raises its ugly head, and the terrifying future she thought she'd evaded becomes a reality—one that seems impossible to escape.

In the final chapter, *Redemption*, Jewel is rescued from Bangkok's evil flesh markets by a covert government agency. Haunted by her last memories of Annie, Jewel vows to do whatever it takes to find her friend—hopefully in time to save her from Gregory's sadistic and murderous intentions. In her new position as an embassy hostess, Jewel forms alliances with political attaches and power brokers, hoping one of them can help her find Annie—still alive.

World Without Love contains mature content
and is intended for an 18+ audience

World Without Love–**The Complete Series** is available
in eBook at **WorldWithoutLove.com**

The New Girl in Town
And Other Journeys Above and Below the Belt

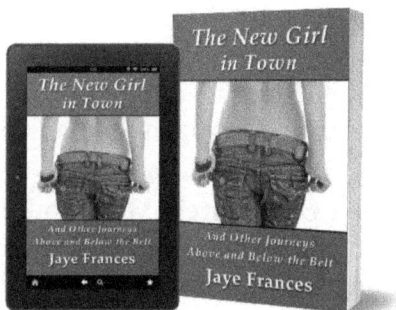

This special collection contains nine of Jaye's most heart-wrenching, mind-tingling, titillating, and thought-provoking stories. Here's a glimpse of what's inside …

- **Our Girl** – Every town has one, and there's always one guy who wants her for his own

- **Three Conversations** – Hindsight often brings wisdom, self-discovery, and a sense of closure—unless the heartache is too much to bear.

- **My First Girlfriend** – There's nothing like a first experience, especially when it brings respect, admiration, and unconditional surrender.

- **The Family Business** – Like mother, like daughter. Until the situation creates a dangerous legacy – and things have to change.

- **The Sighting** – Coming face-to-face with an urban myth can be exciting – and frightening. But when the truth reveals a surprise no one saw coming, it's time for a whole new perspective.

- **Avocados and Fruit Salad** – New beginnings are all around us, if we're willing to recognize the opportunities and take a few risks

- **Younger by Ten** – When love is about the numbers, a few hearts are bound to be broken, especially when you realize your choice of lover had nothing to do with you.

- **A Lie I Desperately Want to Believe** – Trust is often part of the collateral damage when the unquestioning bond of marriage is ripped to shreds.

- **The New Girl in Town** – Sometimes it takes a while to figure out what you want – and build the confidence to go for it!

The New Girl in Town is available in eBook and paperback at **TheNewGirlBook.com**

The Beach

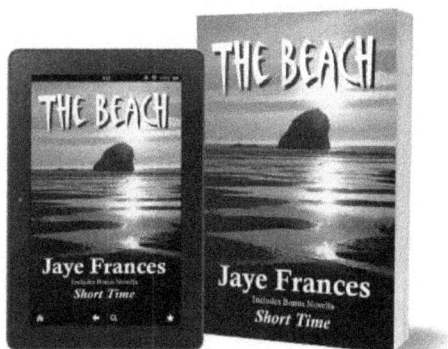

Alan loves the beach. More than a weekend respite, it is his home, his refuge, his sanctuary. And for most of the year, he strolls the sand in blissful solitude, letting nature—and no one else—touch him. But spring has given way to summer, and soon, the annual invasion of vacationers and tourists will subdivide the beach with blankets, umbrellas, and chairs, depriving Alan of his privacy and seclusion—the fundamental touchstones of his life.

Resigned to endure another seasonal onslaught of beach-goers, Alan believes there is nothing he can do but prepare for the worst.

But fate has other plans.

Delivered to him on the crest of a rogue wave, the strange object appears to have no purpose, no practical use—until Alan accidentally discovers what waits inside. Now he must attempt to unravel an ageless mystery, unaware that the final outcome will change his life, and the beach, forever.

In the companion novella *Short Time,* you'll meet a respectable but bored middle-class executive, who exchanges his future for six months of excess and extravagance, only to discover out the price he must pay for his hedonistic indulgence is beyond anything he could have imagined.

The Beach is available in eBook and paperback
at **BewareTheBeach.com**

The Kure

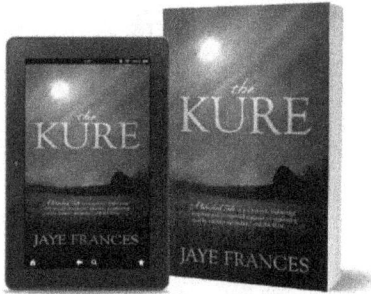

John Tyler, a young man in his early twenties, awakens to find a ghastly affliction taking over his body. When the village doctor offers the conventional, and potentially disfiguring, treatment as the only cure, John tenaciously convinces the doctor to reveal an alternative remedy—a forbidden ritual contained within an ancient manuscript called the *Kure*.

Although initially rejecting the vile and sinister rite, John realizes, too late, that the ritual is more than a faded promise scrawled on a page of crumbling paper. And as cure quickly becomes curse, the demonic text unleashes a dark power that drives him to consider the unthinkable—a depraved and wicked act requiring the corruption of an innocent soul.

The Kure contains mature content
and is intended for an 18+ audience

The Kure is available in eBook and paperback at
TheKureBook.com

Love Travels Forever

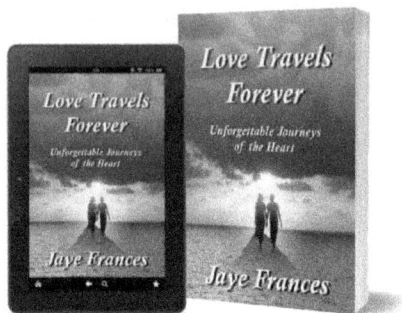

In *Love Travels Forever*, Jaye Frances captures the reader's heart with an inspiring collection of seventeen stories filled with romance and passion, the hopeful innocence of youth, and a love so strong that it transcends the mortality of life. Here are just a few of the people you'll meet:

Evan and Frankie, a loving couple traveling through life hand-in-hand, are unaware that the shadow of fate is about to tear them apart. Helpless to change their shortened future together, one of them makes a promise—a promise of devotion and courage, honoring a love that surpasses the boundaries of time.

Mark and Janice, the perfect couple with the perfect life, are on the threshold of finally seeing their dreams come true—until an unexpected circumstance changes their lives forever.

Danny, a young soldier fresh out of boot-camp, is desperate to find a way to travel home and marry his sweetheart before being shipped overseas.

Stranded in a train station on a three day pass with no hope in sight, Danny meets Wanda, an incredible woman who vows to find a way to bring Danny and his fiance together.

Nora and Georgia are two eight-year-old best friends who share giggles, dolls, and secrets. But when one of them faces sudden danger, the other responds with an unconditional act of love and forges a lifelong bond between them unaffected by fear or prejudice.

So find a quiet spot, get comfy, and grab a box of tissue. You're about to take an unforgettable journey of the heart, to a place where compassion and hope have no limits, and where love continues to travel forever.

Love Travels Forever is available in eBook & paperback at **LoveTravelsForever.com**

Jaye Frances Books are Available in eBook
and Paperback at:

JayeFrancesBooks.com

JayeFrances.com

www.ingramcontent.com/pod-product-compliance
Lightning Source LLC
Chambersburg PA
CBHW031318040426
42443CB00005B/117